DID YOU KNOW?

Tiger

DID YOU KNOW?
Tiger
young
reed

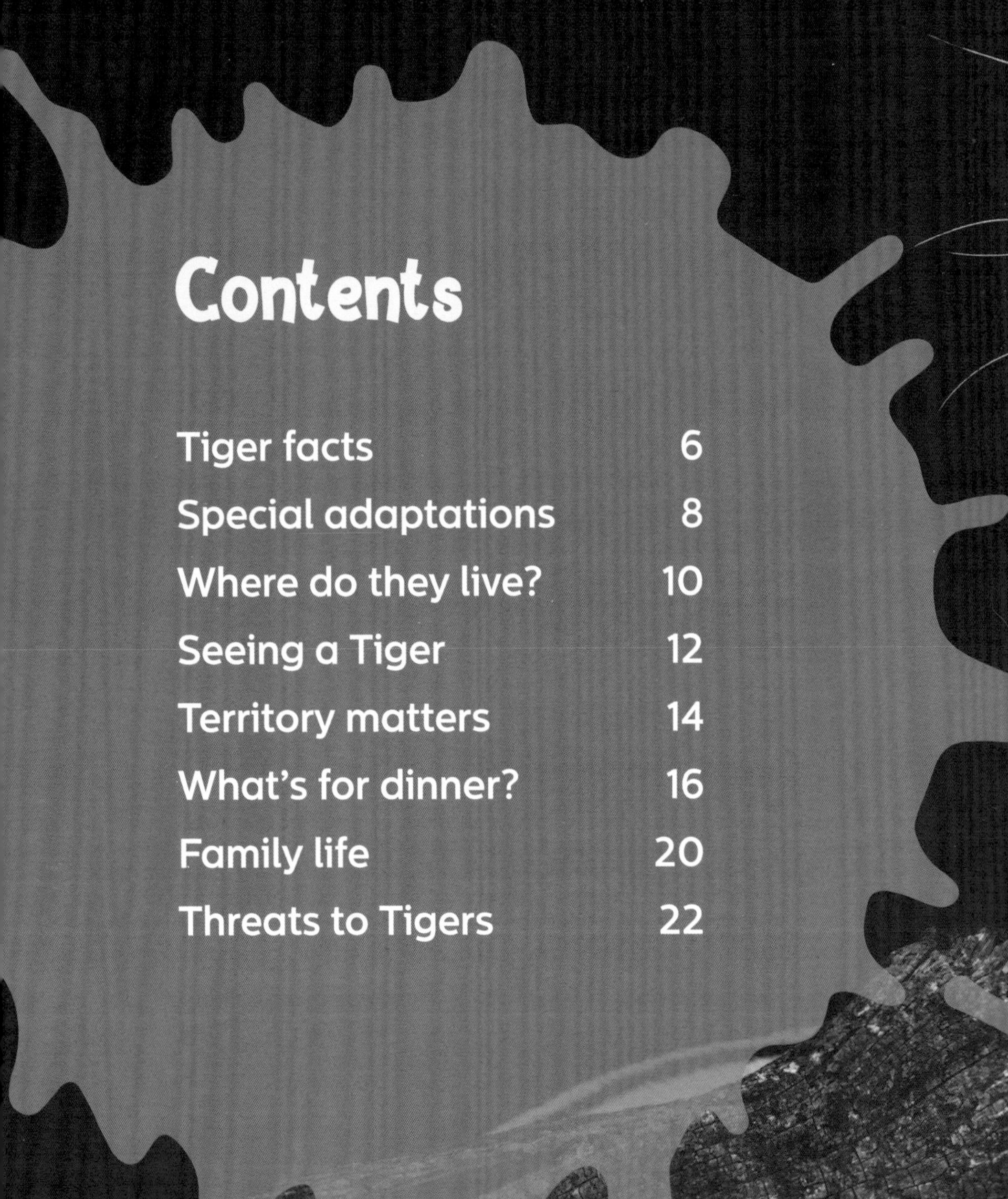

Contents

Tiger facts

- Tigers are **big cats**. They are related to the common pet moggy, but measuring up to **three metres** in length they will not fit through a cat-flap!
- They are **apex predators**, meaning that they are at the top of the food chain.
- Being primarily **nocturnal**, they are most active and do most of their hunting at night.
- Unlike domestic cats, Tigers love going for a **swim**.

Snow Leopard

- The Tiger's closest living relative is thought to be the **Snow Leopard**.

Special adaptations

- A Tiger's **stripes** work as **camouflage**, helping to hide it in long grass so that it can stalk its prey.
- Tiger feet have **soft pads**, which help them to walk quietly, and long **retractable claws** that pop out when needed to catch dinner.
- Their long, sharp **teeth** are typical of a **carnivore** that eats meat.

● These predators are powerfully built and the long tail helps with balance while chasing prey at high speed.

Where do they live?

- Traditionally, wild Tigers had a huge range across the whole of **Asia**, including much of Central Asia, India, South-East Asia, Indonesia, China, Korea and eastern Russia.

- They inhabited hot and humid rainforests, freezing tundra, and many other habitats in between. About one hundred years ago there were estimated to be **one hundred thousand** wild Tigers in the world.

Former range
Current range

● However, as the human population has increased exponentially, people have hunted these cats and destroyed their habitat, meaning that Tigers have become **extinct** across most of their former range.

Seeing a Tiger

- Today all that remains is a remnant population of perhaps **less than four thousand** wild Tigers; the majority of these are in **India**.

- Thankfully, many of these animals are protected in special reserves, so it is still possible to watch Tigers in their natural habitat in a few places.
- Captive Tigers are a familiar sight in zoos and animal parks around the world, where they have become a favourite attraction for millions of people.
- There are thought to be about fifteen thousand Tigers in captivity around the world – nearly four times as many as remain in the wild.

Territory matters

- The size of a Tiger's territory depends on how much food is available. It can vary from **five square kilometres** in India to **five hundred square kilometres** in Russia.

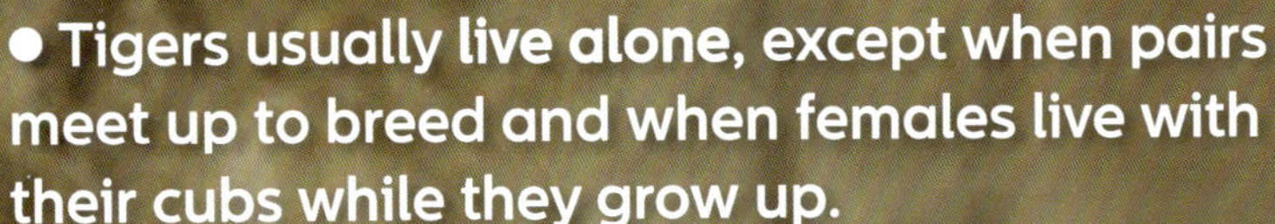

- Tigers usually live alone, except when pairs meet up to breed and when females live with their cubs while they grow up.
- These cats mark their territory using scent and by scratching marks on trees, just like a pet cat does.

What's for dinner?

- Tigers are **carnivores**, meaning that they feed mostly on meat.

- In the wild, deer and wild boar are popular prey items, but Tigers will also hunt and eat smaller animals and birds.

• Farm animals such as sheep and goats will also be taken, bringing Tigers into conflict with humans.

- A Tiger might travel up to **twenty kilometres** in a night in search of food.
- Typically a Tiger has more than **ten unsuccessful hunting attempts** before it makes a kill.

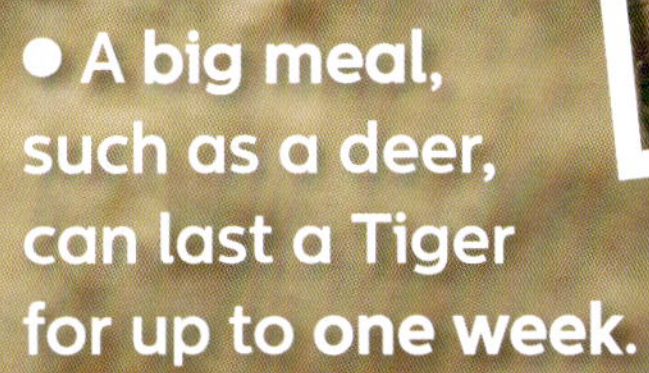

- **A big meal,** such as a deer, can last a Tiger for up to **one week.**

Family life

- Baby Tigers are born in a **litter** of up to **four cubs.** They live in a **den** for their first two months.
- When born the cubs are **blind** for the first few days, and they rely on their **mother's milk** for the first six months of life.
- The young stay with mum for about **two years,** learning how to hunt and fend for themselves.

Threats to Tigers

- Tigers are listed as **Endangered** – there may be less than **four thousand** left in the wild in the whole of Asia.
- This situation is entirely down to us **humans**. The natural habitat available for Tigers to live in is shrinking because of increasing human populations causing **deforestation**.
- Humans have **hunted** Tigers for centuries, and this still happens, especially when the big cats come into conflict with us by preying on domestic animals.
- Adult Tigers have no natural predators, but other large carnivores such as **Wolves** and **Sloth Bears** may be a threat to Tiger cubs.

First published in 2025 by New Holland Publishers
Sydney

newhollandpublishers.com

A record of this book is held at the National Library of Australia.

ISBN 9781760798024

OTHER TITLES IN THE 'DID YOU KNOW?' SERIES:

Dolphins
ISBN 9781760798000

Kangaroos
ISBN 9781921073861

Koala
ISBN 9781921073878

Lizards
ISBN 9781921073885

Meerkat
ISBN 9781921073892

Monkeys
ISBN 9781760798031

Penguins
ISBN 9781921073908

Red Panda
ISBN 9781921073915

Sharks
ISBN 9781760798017

For details of these books and hundreds of other Natural History titles see newhollandpublishers.com